HOMES

IN HOT AND COLD PLACES

SIMON CRISP

Wayland

TITLES IN THIS SERIES

Animals in Hot and Cold Places
Clothes in Hot and Cold Places
Food and Farming in Hot and Cold Places
Homes in Hot and Cold Places

Series editor: Geraldine Purcell
Series designer: Helen White

Cover: (top) An Inuit building a fire at the entrance to his igloo.
(bottom) This building in Greece is painted white to reflect the heat
of the sun's rays.
Title page: An Inuit building an igloo from blocks of snow.

First published in 1994 by Wayland (Publishers) Limited
61 Western Road, Hove, East Sussex BN3 1JD

British Library Cataloguing in Publication Data
Crisp, Simon
  Homes in Hot and Cold Places. – (Hot & Cold Series)
  I. Title II. Price, David III. Series 643

ISBN 0 7502 0716 7

Typeset by White Design
Printed and bound in Great Britain by BPCC Paulton Books Ltd., Paulton

CONTENTS

INTRODUCTION

The planet Earth is our home. Not everyone who lives here lives in the same sort of place or in the same sort of way. We live in many different parts of the Earth. Some of us live in large cities and towns; others live in small villages in the countryside.

The houses that we live in are also our homes. These can be very big with lots of rooms and lots of people. Or a home can be just one room where a person lives all on his or her own.

Places near the North and South Poles are very cold and may have snow all year. People who have homes in cold places need houses that will keep them warm. They have to heat their houses and then keep the heat in. The hottest places on the Earth are near the Equator. People who have homes in hot places need houses that will keep the sun's heat out. But they still need to use heat to cook food, heat water and keep warm at night.

▼ **People who live in very cold parts of the world, such as the Antarctic, need homes that will protect them from the snow and icy wind.**

◄ **If you lived on a hot, tropical island, such as in the Maldives in the Indian Ocean, you would need a home that would shelter you from the hot sun and provide cool shade.**

ARCTIC

EQUATOR

ANTARCTIC

In between the Poles and the Equator are places that are not so hot or so cold. These places are where most people live. Their homes need to be suitable for the different temperatures and weather conditions that occur in the different seasons of the year.

AROUND THE HOME
The following text mentions some hot and cold items used around the home. Can you think of any others?

HOT THINGS CAN BE FOUND UPSTAIRS
Some people warm their beds at night with an electric blanket. Have you got a hot-water bottle for your bed?

Some people use heated tongs or curlers to make their hair wavy. Drying your hair is faster with a hair dryer. If clothes cannot dry on a washing line outside they may be kept in a warm airing cupboard.

HOT AND COLD IN THE BATHROOM
Keeping clean is an important part of being healthy.

Bathrooms have hot and cold water for washing. On a hot day you may like to take a cool bath or shower. A warm bath is a great way to get clean and to relax.

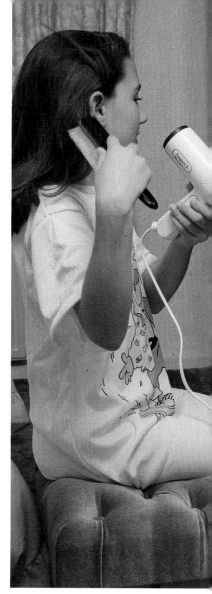

▲ This girl is drying her hair with a hair dryer in her bedroom.

◄ Bathing in a warm bubble bath is lots of fun.

► Washing machines use hot and cold water to wash clothes.

COOL FOOD

Keeping food cool helps it to stay fresher for longer. Most houses have refrigerators, which keep food at 5°C. Even colder temperatures are used to keep food for a long time. This is called freezing. Sometimes frozen food needs to be defrosted before it is used.

HOT AND COLD IN THE KITCHEN

Heat is used in the kitchen a lot. Some people have washing machines in their homes which are often kept in the kitchen. A washing machine uses hot or warm

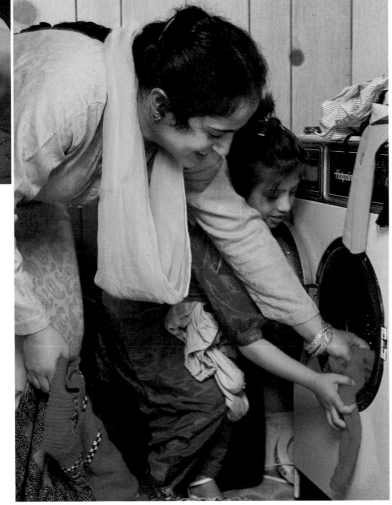

water to wash clothes. Clothes have labels on them which tell you at which temperature they should be washed. Find out which clothes are washed best at low or high temperatures. After they are washed, clothes are sometimes dried in a special drying machine or on a washing line. After this they may be pressed with a hot iron.

Some food needs to be cooked by heat in a hot oven. After food is eaten the dishes have to be washed. Some homes have dishwashers, but most dishes are washed by hand in warm water in the sink.

TEMPERATURE AND

▲ Most of these huts in Lesotho, southern Africa, do not have windows so that the hot sun's rays cannot get in and therefore the huts keep cool.

Is it hot or cold outside? In countries that lie between the Equator and the North or South Poles the weather can change during different seasons of the year. In winter it may be cold or it may snow. In summer it is likely to be warm and perhaps sunny. In order to measure just how hot or cold it is outside we need to know the temperature. We measure temperature by using a thermometer. A thermometer has a series of numbers called a scale. When the temperature is 0°C outside, it is so cold that water freezes and there can be snow. At 20°C the climate is warm outside and at 40°C it is very hot.

CLIMATE

In winter temperatures are usually at their lowest. During summer temperatures are usually at their highest. Of course, what seems like summer to an Inuit living close to the North Pole region would seem colder than the coldest winter to someone from an island in the Indian Ocean.

▶ **This Inuit village is on the shores of the freezing Arctic Ocean.**

BUILDING A HOT OR COLD HOUSE

Houses give us protection from the weather outside and can be made of many different kinds of material. What is your house made of: bricks, concrete or wood? In hot places like Central Africa houses may be made of mud. When mud is baked in the sun it becomes hard like brick. Mud bricks are cheap and strong and can last hundreds of years. Other houses may be made from reeds and grasses which are woven tightly together. These houses are waterproof and also

▼ These houses near Lake Titicaca, Peru, are built from dried reeds, woven tightly together. Rain runs off the reed roofs and the houses keep warm and dry.

◀ **Some of these houses in Turkey have been built into the mounds of rock.**

act as a shade from the hot sun. In waterlogged, marshy places reed houses can actually float on the water. Long poles buried deep in the riverbed stop them floating away.

In cold places such as northern Canada and Scandinavia houses are usually made from strong wood and concrete. Wooden houses stay warm because it is difficult for heat to escape through wooden walls.

People around the world build houses out of materials which are close by and easy to get. In areas of the Middle East and in North Africa some people live in caves. The caves are cool inside because the sun's rays cannot get in. At night these cave dwellers may light fires to keep themselves warm.

MOVABLE HOMES

◄ This hut has been built on to a sledge. It can be pulled by a team of reindeer and moved from one hunting area to another in Russia.

▼ This Inuit is building an igloo from blocks of snow.

Some people do not live in one place all the year round but travel long distances. They do this to find places where there are better supplies of food and water or better weather. Travelling people often carry their homes with them or build homes in places where they decide to settle for a while.

Most Inuit now live in big towns or permanent villages, but many still travel across their frozen land on hunting trips. To keep warm they build igloos – shelters made from blocks of solid snow. An igloo can be built in an hour by an experienced Inuit. Flaming lamps warm the igloo but the snow does not melt because it is so hard and cold.

In the past some groups of native Americans used to live in tepees. These tepees were usually made of buffalo skin. Several skins were sewn together. These were then lifted on to poles and tied together at the top. Other poles were used to form a hole to let smoke out of the top if the fire inside got too smoky.

▲ **TOP**
This traditional Cree tent in Canada has been made by stretching material over a dome-shaped structure made from poles.

▲ **ABOVE**
Some modern camping tents are very similar to the Cree tent.

HOT AND COLD HOUSES:

▼ The blinds on the windows of these houses in Spain can be rolled up or down to keep the hot sunshine out or let a cool breeze inside.

Houses come in all shapes and sizes. The design of a house or block of flats can help keep them warm or cool. Many people in both hot and cold countries build houses with thick walls. In hot places thick walls stop the sun's rays from getting in, so the house is cool. In cold places thick walls stop the heat from fires or radiators escaping.

In Mediterranean countries, such as Greece and Spain, some houses are built facing into a courtyard, where there is always some shade. The windows facing the outside are usually small, so not much heat gets in but breezes can blow through to keep the houses cool. In hot countries buildings with large windows often have shutters. These allow the breeze through but keep the sun's rays and insects out.

In Indonesia and Malaysia some houses are built on stilts. This stops them from being flooded during the rainy season. Also, breezes can blow under and around the houses which helps keep them cool.

DESIGN DIFFERENCES

In warm places people spend much of their time outside. A lot of houses in rural USA have porches where people can sit. These are usually in the shade of the house. In places where it stays warm even at night houses often have flat roofs. People sleep on the roof in the cooler night air.

The design of roofs is also important in cold countries. Some houses have almost flat roofs. In winter snow lies on the roof for months. This acts as a blanket keeping the heat in. However, in most snowy places roofs are steep, so that snow and rain will run off.

▶ **This chalet in Switzerland has a sloping roof so that the thick layer of snow will slide off before it gets too heavy and damages the roof.**

HEATING A HOME

FOSSIL FUELS AND BIOMASS
Houses in cold countries need to be warm inside. This usually involves burning a fuel. Anything that burns is a fuel. The main fuels used in developed countries are fossil fuels such as coal, gas or oil and nuclear power.

These fuels are used in power stations to make electricity. The heat from burning the fuel makes steam. The steam turns a turbine

▲ **This girl in Morocco has collected dried brushwood to use as fuel.**

▶ **This Laplander herder has made a fire from wood cut from the forest around his hunting hut in Norway.**

to produce electricity. How many things can you think of which use electricity to make heat in your home?

The major problem with fossil fuels is that they are being used up and cannot be replaced. Many people think that the world's resources of oil and gas will run out within fifty years. Coal may last for about 250 years. We need to save energy to make the resources of fossil fuels last longer.

In developing countries many people get heat by burning plants such as wood, straw or sugar-cane. These fuels are called biomass. In some areas of rural Ireland peat is burnt on open fires. A peat fire can burn for a long time and is used to heat the houses and to cook food.

Unlike fossil fuels, biomass can be renewed. When fuel runs out farmers can grow more. Wood can be replaced by planting more trees, grass can be replaced by planting more grass and so on. In the future more countries may have to use biomass for fuel when resources of oil, gas and coal run low.

▼ **Fossil fuels such as gas and coal are burnt in power stations to produce electricity. The electricity is then used in our homes for heating and lighting.**

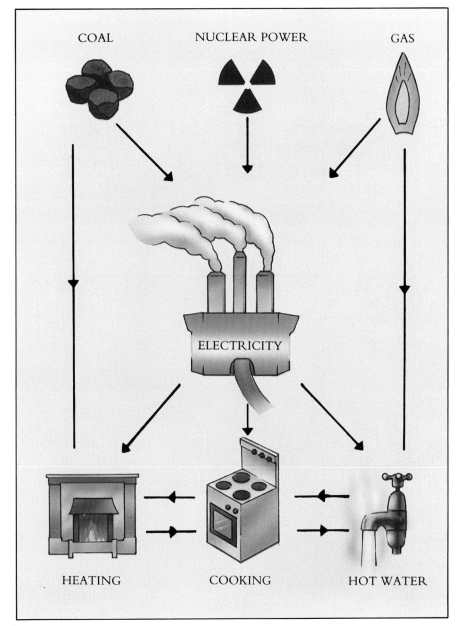

COAL NUCLEAR POWER GAS

ELECTRICITY

HEATING COOKING HOT WATER

SOLAR ENERGY

There are ways to heat a home that do not involve burning fuels. One is to use heat from the sun. This is called solar energy. Most people use this at some time. Drying clothes on a line on a sunny day is an example of using the heat from the sun.

Places with lots of sunshine each day can use solar energy in a special way. This is done by using solar cells, which turn the energy from the sun into electricity. Electricity can then be used for heating and cooking. Some houses have solar panels fixed on the roofs or walls. The panels contain pipes filled with water. The sun heats up the water.

The hot water can be used straight away or it can be stored in tanks to be used later when the sun is not shining.

Solar power does not cause pollution and will not run out like fossil fuels. But it is only useful in places where there is a lot of sunshine. Even in a sunny place a solar power station, which could supply electricity to a city, would have to be enormous and have thousands of solar panels.

▲ These solar panels produce the heating and power for this hotel in the Himalayas.

▼ How a solar panel works.

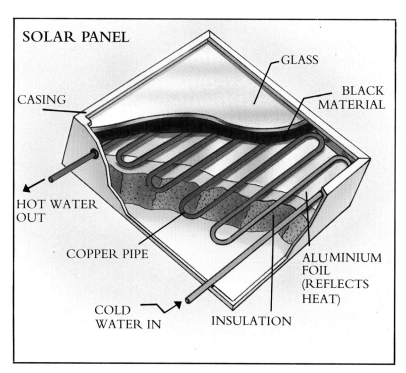

SOLAR PANEL

GLASS

CASING

BLACK MATERIAL

HOT WATER OUT

COPPER PIPE

ALUMINIUM FOIL (REFLECTS HEAT)

COLD WATER IN

INSULATION

GEOTHERMAL ENERGY

It is extremely hot deep inside the Earth. This heat is called geothermal heat and at some places it comes very close to the surface or even bursts out of the Earth, for example at a volcano. It is too difficult and dangerous to use the heat from a volcano to heat houses, but in Iceland, New Zealand and Japan people do use geothermal energy. These countries have hot springs where water is heated underground by geothermal energy. It is possible to drill down into the Earth and run heated water along pipes. The steam this creates can be used in power stations to make electricity. The main problem with geothermal energy is that it is only available in a few places on Earth.

▼ **This Japanese boy is using an outdoor bath which is heated by geothermal energy.**

COOLING A HOME

As well as the design, there are other ways of keeping a house cool. One is to paint the building white. Darker colours absorb (take in) the sun's heat. White reflects more of the heat, so white walls are cooler than dark ones.

On a warm day our bodies stay cool by sweating. The sweat takes heat away from our bodies, but it heats the surrounding air. If we are inside we need a breeze, perhaps from an open window, to move this warm air away so that we can sweat properly and stay cool.

In many hot places a breeze is created indoors by a fan. A fan is usually operated by electricity which moves

▼ **These houses in Greece have been painted white to reflect the sun's heat.**

FAN BLADES TURN

AIR CIRCULATES

▲ The blades of the fans move the air, which makes a cooling breeze

▼ This underground house in Iran has air holes built into the walls to allow cool breezes into the house.

a blade, or set of blades, which in turn moves the air around. This allows cooler and fresher air to circulate around a room and makes it more comfortable for the people inside.

In developed countries, such as the USA, many homes and offices have air conditioning. Air is cooled or warmed as it flows through the air conditioning system and is then blown around a room or building. Air conditioning keeps the temperature at a steady and comfortable level for the people inside. Unfortunately, air conditioning is expensive and uses a lot of electricity.

KEEPING HOUSES WARM

If you can stop the heat escaping, a house stays warm. Once a house is warm it does not need to be heated as much, so less fuel is burnt. This saves energy. The world's resources of fossil fuels are running out and the more energy we can save the longer they will last.

When it is cold outside, you wrap yourself up to keep your body heat in. In the same way a house can be wrapped up. This is called insulation. Insulation traps hot air inside. We cannot put a big coat around a house but we can use other ways to keep heat inside. For example we can put up curtains over the windows.

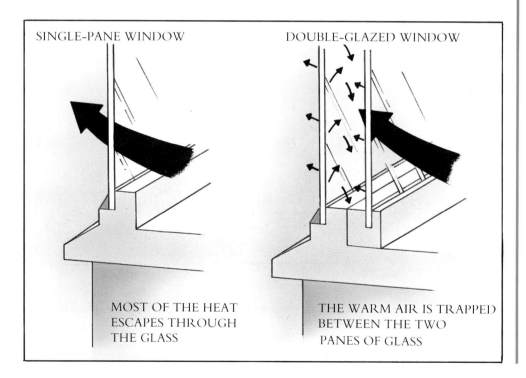

SINGLE-PANE WINDOW

DOUBLE-GLAZED WINDOW

MOST OF THE HEAT ESCAPES THROUGH THE GLASS

THE WARM AIR IS TRAPPED BETWEEN THE TWO PANES OF GLASS

◀ **Double glazing helps to keep a house warm because the air trapped between the two panes of glass helps to keep the heat inside.**

◀ These homes in Iceland are covered with grass turf to stop the heat escaping through the roof.

Some homes have double glazing – windows which have two panes of glass instead of one. The space between the panes stops the heat getting out. Carpets help to stop the heat from going through the floorboards.

Hot air rises so most heat in a house heads for the roof. It can be trapped there if the house has loft insulation. Loft insulation can be made from materials such as fibreglass or special wool. If it has been snowing during winter you can tell which houses in a street have good loft insulation by looking at the roofs. If a roof is covered in snow it means the heat from the inside of the house is not escaping, but if there is no snow at all then that means the hot air is rising through the roof and is melting the snow.

PROJECT BOX

How can you save energy in your home?

The easiest way is to stop draughts. Check your house and find the draughtiest places. Some of the places to check are fireplaces, floorboards, windows, around the doors and the letter box. Can you think of ways to stop the draughts? Ask an adult to help you.

CENTRAL HEATING: PAST AND PRESENT

▼ You can see the hypocaust under the floor of this Roman building. Fires were lit underground and the hot air rose up the channels and heated the floor.

We need warmth to feel comfortable and to stay healthy. If a person gets too cold they may suffer from hypothermia. Every year during winter thousands of old people die around the world because their homes get too cold.

An electric or open fire can heat one room, but in many houses and flats one heater can warm rooms all over the house. This is called central heating. In Roman times wealthy people's houses were heated by a fire under the floors. The fire was controlled so that the house did not catch alight. Hot air from the fire was channelled under the house and up through slits in the floor to keep the rooms warm. The air channels were called the hypocaust.

▼ You can see the hypocaust under the floor of this Roman building. Fires were lit underground and the hot air rose up the channels and heated the floor.

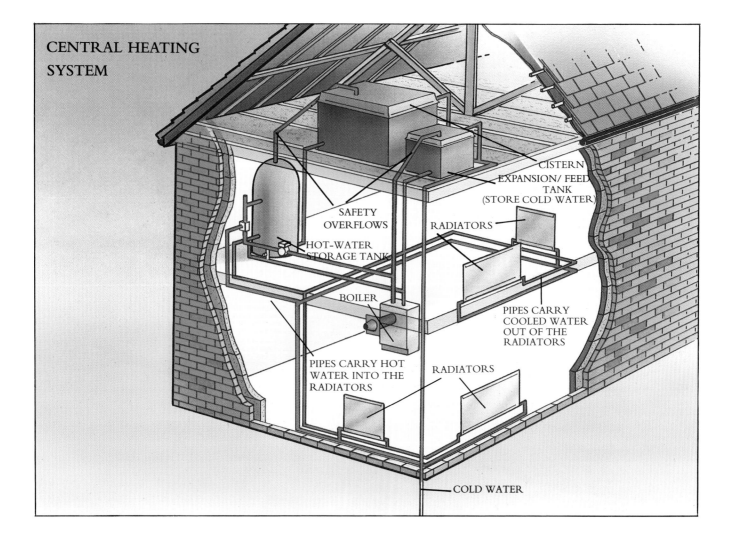

CENTRAL HEATING SYSTEM

CISTERN EXPANSION/ FEED TANK (STORE COLD WATER)

SAFETY OVERFLOWS

RADIATORS

HOT-WATER STORAGE TANK

BOILER

PIPES CARRY COOLED WATER OUT OF THE RADIATORS

PIPES CARRY HOT WATER INTO THE RADIATORS

RADIATORS

COLD WATER

In modern central heating a hot liquid is used instead of air. The liquid (usually water or oil) is heated by a boiler. Then it is pumped through pipes to radiators in different parts of the house. The radiators then give out heat to the different rooms. The amount of heat given off is controlled by a thermostat. The thermostat turns the heater off when the liquid gets too hot. Then the liquid cools. When it gets too cool the thermostat turns the heater on again. This way the radiators stay at the temperature you want.

▲ **This is a diagram of the central heating system of a house.**

HOT AND COLD IN THE KITCHEN

Most of the equipment in a kitchen uses heat, such as the cooker and the boiler that heats the water for the hot water tap. In some homes the kitchen is a separate room used specially for cooking.

▲ **This woman in Nepal is using straw as fuel for the cooking stove.**

THE COOKER

In many houses in Scandinavia and Canada people use wood-burning stoves. These act as ovens to cook food and also heat the water and warm the entire house.

Whatever type of stove is used, it must use heat to cook food. Some foods need to be cooked to kill the bacteria (small germs) in them otherwise we could become ill. Other foods simply taste better when they are heated up.

THE REFRIGERATOR

Some foods and drinks taste better when they are cold and these can be kept chilled in a refrigerator.

It is important to keep raw food cold because bacteria make poisons which spoil the food. Bacteria do not spread so quickly in the cold. The cooler the food is kept in a refrigerator the longer it will last. For example milk will keep fresh for one day at 10°C, but for two days at 5°C.

WASHING-UP
Most kitchens have a sink with hot and cold water. After a meal dishes need to be washed so that they can be used again. Using hot water makes it easier to clean the dishes properly.

THE WASHING MACHINE
In many developing countries clothes are washed by hand either in a sink or in a nearby stream. The clothes are cleaned thoroughly and then left to dry in the open air. In developed countries many houses and flats have washing machines which are usually kept in the kitchen. Washing machines use a lot of electricity and hot water but save a lot of time. After clothes have been washed and dried they are often ironed. A steam iron uses hot water to help press clothes.

▲ Refrigerators keep food fresh.
▼ These people are washing their clothes in a stream in Morocco.

HOT AND COLD

▲ **Taking a hot or warm bath keeps us clean and healthy.**

Do you have a bath or a shower in your house? Perhaps you have both, or neither. Having a separate room in the house for bathing is quite a modern idea. In the past most people did not bathe at home so there was no need for a bathroom. People would wash using water from wells, rivers or even the sea.

When people started to bathe in the home it was usually in a tub in front of the fire. The tub was filled with water heated on the stove or fire.

Many homes in developing countries do not have bathrooms, mainly because the climate is warm enough for people to wash in rivers and streams. Many other homes do have bathrooms, especially in houses in the cities. Taking a bath in hot water keeps you clean and smelling nice, and is a way to relax.

The idea of a separate bathroom is not so new in Finland. For 1,000 years the Finns have had special bathrooms called saunas. In a sauna you sit on wooden benches. The air is heated to 80°C to make you sweat. The sweat leaving the body cleans the pores of the skin. After a short while you take a cold bath.

IN THE BATHROOM

After the cold bath you sit in the hot sauna again, followed by another cold bath. This continues until you feel clean and relaxed. Nowadays saunas are found all over the world.

Turkish baths are similar to saunas. Turkish baths have a steam room. After you have sweated for a while an attendant washes you with warm water and soap. This is followed by a massage to get the muscles to relax. Afterwards you can have a cold shower.

▼ **This is an old drawing of a Turkish bath in Istanbul, Turkey.**

GLOSSARY

biomass Plants such as wood and straw which are used as an energy source (fuel).

defrosted When frozen food is removed from a freezer to return to room temperature until all the ice has melted. It is very important to defrost uncooked food thoroughly before it is cooked.

Equator An imaginary line making a circle around the Earth halfway between the North and South Poles.

fossil fuels Sources of energy such as oil, gas and coal which are made from the bodies of dead animals and plants (fossils) which were left in the earth millions of years ago.

geothermal The heat from deep inside the Earth. Power can be made from the steam produced by this heat.

hypothermia The illness caused when the body's temperature falls below the normal level, usually 36.9°C.

nuclear power The energy released when atoms are split. Atoms are tiny particles, too small to be seen, of which all things are made up. Nuclear power can be used in power stations to produce electricity.

peat Soil made from rotted down plants. The soil can be dried and used as a fuel.

Poles The two regions which are at the most northerly and southerly points of the Earth.

radiators Metal covered panels containing pipes through which steam or hot water pass and heat the air in different rooms.

reflects When light shines off a surface.

rural The countryside.

seasons The four parts of the year – spring, summer, autumn and winter – which have different temperature and weather conditions.

solar energy Power that has been made by using the energy from the sun. The sun's rays heat liquid, usually water, which in turn produces steam that turns a turbine in a power station.

thermostat A machine that controls the temperature in a heating system.

turbine An engine which forces wheels or blades to move around.

FURTHER READING

Bioenergy Graham Houghton, (Wayland, 1990)

Geothermal Energy Graham Rickard, (Wayland, 1990)

Indians of the Plains Ruth Thompson, (Franklin Watts, 1991)

Solar Energy Graham Rickard, (Wayland, 1990)

The Young Green Consumer Guide Elkington & Hailes, (Victor Gollancz, 1990)

PICTURE ACKNOWLEDGEMENTS

Bryan & Cherry Alexander *cover* (top), *title page*, 9, 12-13, 13 (top), 16 (bottom); Chapel Studios 27 (top) (T. Richardson); Sue Cunningham Photographic 6 (bottom); C.M. Dixon 24; Mary Evans Picture Library 29; Eye Ubiquitous *cover* (bottom), 6-7 (top) (R. Chester), 13 (bottom right) (J. Burke), 18 (top) (D. Cumming); Explorer 22-3 (Page); Geoscience Features Picture Library 11; The Hutchison Library 21 (D. Baldwin); Life File 27 (bottom) (P. James); Link 19 (M. Longley); Christine Osborne Pictures 16 (top); Still Pictures 26 (J. Schytte); Tony Stone Worldwide 4 (R. Mear), 5 (P. Seaward), 8 (N. DeVore), 10 (R. Smith), 15; Survival Anglia 12 (R. & J. Kemp); Wayland Picture Library 7 (bottom), 20, 28; ZEFA 14 (W. Ostgathe). All artwork by David Price.

INDEX

Numbers in **bold** indicate entries which are illustrated.